Debt FREE and Loving it!

Your how to guide for a happy & debt free life

Sarah W.

Contents

Sporty new cars, big elaborate houses, designer clothes, sparkling diamonds, and a magnificent house on the beach! Joining the country club, staying in 5-star hotels, traveling abroad, and enrolling your kids in the finest private schools. And when you can't afford it any longer, there's always "Mastercard"!

Ah, now that's the good life!

Or is it?

Today's world is so focused on immediate gratification and hyperconsumerism that many people have forgotten how to enjoy life. They don't even know how to slow down and enjoy the simple things in life that can give so much more meaning and fulfillment to their lives.

People are spending an inordinate amount of time at their jobs and they're constantly scrambling to keep up. That leaves little time left over for family and friends – and they certainly don't have time left over for themselves! Many have abandoned their personal values for the sake of "appearing wealthy". Their vital capacities of life are suffering and they don't even realize it is happening.

In a world where spending tomorrow's earnings and cash has become the norm, it's hard to imagine a life with financial, mental, physical and spiritual peace. But don't be fooled. Simplifying your life and living a 'better life' that is filled with purpose is just at your fingertips. And all it requires is taking control of your finances and your vital capacities of life.

Unfortunately, most people don't know how to slow down long enough to take control of their own lives though. They continue on the treadmill and rat-race of life day in and day out – experiencing little joy and fulfillment with where and how they spend their time. They're so busy trying to keep up with everyone else, that they lose themselves and their own identity in a sea of faces.

Today's "I've got to have it now" mentality is robbing tens of thousands of people from enjoying life. The stress and anxiety from being over-worked and loaded with debt takes a toll – yet they keep on doing what they are doing.

And if they keep on doing what they are doing, they'll keep on getting what they have been getting – deeper in debt and more stressed!

Isn't it time to make a change?

Uncovering today's world of materialism

Consumerism today is all about 'he who has the most possessions wins'! Unfortunately there is a widespread mindset that more 'things' will make you happier, make people like you better, and lead to a better and more fulfilled life.

Think about the things that turn heads and have people talking. Consider the things that create the impression of money and wealth. Outward appearances can be deceiving, but we soon forget that important fact.

❖ New cars are a major status symbol in today's society. Cars today come with a hefty price tag and when you buy a car with all of the bells and whistles, you are perceived to be 'wealthy'. But along with that status symbol comes a 4, 5, or even 6 year payment plan. The more you pay on that shiny new automobile, the more it depreciates. And your debt builds.

❖ Housing is a major status symbol for the majority of people in today's society. Living in the 'right neighborhood' is an important part of buying a new house. Most people seem to believe that the bigger the house, the better – and the perception again is that wealthy people live in big houses. But along with the big house, comes a mega mortgage! Too many people are 'house poor' with mortgage payments out of control.

❖ Materialism has reached an all time high with most Americans. That is evident through their willingness to sacrifice financial independence and financial security for designer clothes, elaborate home furnishings, expensive jewelry, pleasure boats, seaside vacation homes, and a multitude of other items. Just whip out the plastic cards and it's instant gratification!

> **Americans are actually consumed by consumerism today. Luxuries have now become necessities in the eyes of many. And it is a measure of success to acquire an arsenal of consumer goods for the world to see.**

Possessions have become so important to us that we will go to great lengths to acquire them – and that usually means going into debt or spending tomorrow's earnings. Many people will do whatever it takes for immediate gratification without considering the consequences of tomorrow or next year.

Many people are so obsessed with materialistic things, that they forget what's important in life. If they really stop and take a hard look at their lives, they will probably find that in the process of accumulating possessions, they have forgotten to enjoy their possessions and live life!

They've been too busy figuring out what to buy next and looking at what others have accumulated. Envy, greed, and obsession have created a world where credit cards and materialism are the norm.

The process of building an arsenal of materialistic possessions takes a toll on most people. It can quickly zap their finances – but more importantly, it can erode their mental, physical, and spiritual health as well. The stress and strain of over-spending and focusing on 'things' creates an array of ailments for the average person. That translates to mental and physical ailments and sometimes chronic illness.

There is an outrageous desire to spend money just to outwardly demonstrate that one is wealthy – or at least, perceived to be wealthy. People want to fit in and that often means going beyond their comfort level of spending to do so.

Some of the things that are considered affluent include:

- ❖ Being a member of a prestigious country club
- ❖ Wearing designer clothes
- ❖ Driving the 'right' automobile
- ❖ Attending a private school
- ❖ Living in an impressive neighborhood
- ❖ Being a member of the right 'click'
- ❖ Attending the most recognized social events
- ❖ Traveling to expensive destinations

These are all important goals for many people in today's society. But if people would really stop and look, they may discover that these are not really their goals at all. They are goals that have been influenced and determined by someone else.

They are working hard to climb the ladder to success, but the ladder is leaning against the wrong building. They are working hard to cut down the tree, but the tree is in the wrong forest. Somehow their life has gotten off on the wrong track and they don't even realize how or when it happened.

But worst of all, they don't know how to change. They're scared to think about change and they don't know where to start. They've dug a deep hole and rather than struggling to climb out of the hole, it's just easier to keep digging.

How did we get where we are?

Going beyond your financial resources typically means the use of credit cards and acquiring debt. It is a known fact that people spend more when they use credit cards than when they use cash. Using credit cards is easy and it does not feel like spending 'real money'. But consider that credit cards require you to pay much more for every item you purchase when you use that plastic card! Interest, penalties, and fees accumulate quickly.

Did you realize that according to the American Bankers' Association, the average family today has at least $8,000 in credit card debt?
That's a lot of debt! And they keep on buying and charging and accumulating 'things'!

Ironically, many people who accumulate the most material possessions, including the biggest house and the newest cars, are actually in debt with little hope of financial freedom in the foreseeable future. This contributes to the stress and anxiety for many people and it also leads to mental, spiritual and physical decline in health.

To put it in perspective, consider these facts:[1]

- Consumers have accumulated more than $2.2 trillion in purchases by using major credit cards in the past year.

- Americans have a habit of spending more than they have and it has become an acceptable practice and way of life.

- Credit card debit grew by 315% from 1989 to 2006!

- Less and less people are paying credit card bills on time, piling on interest and penalties to already soaring debt.

- Americans have more debt today than ever before – and growing!

---

[1]

http://www.cnn.com/2008/LIVING/personal/02/22/financial.security/index.html

- Credit cards have become a way of life and way to horde more material possessions than a person can use.

- Buying things without having money is easier today than ever before.

- Students are solicited by credit card companies every day – drawing them into the web of debt.

How did it all happen and what has driven consumers to such lengths that they would jeopardize their financial, physical, and mental health for possessions?

People want to blame someone, or the 'system', or a bad childhood for their situation. They blame their spouse, or their children, or their dog. They blame marketers and TV ads and other promotions. They even blame their employer because they don't get paid enough.

But they're not in their situation because of the money they make. They're in their situation because of the money they SPEND!

Recognizing the problem

What can you do to change your life by creating the life you REALLY want and applying the principle of 'less is more'? That's what we can do for you. Help you see how to become simply happy and debt-free. When you overcome your debt, you will feel an enormous burden lifted and you'll be simply happy!

In a world where most people believe, "I've got to have it now", you can find a place of peace and tranquility by making some changes in your life and by assessing your current situation. You can establish goals that are not focused on money, but focused on a satisfying life. Freedom is within your reach but you have to grasp it and commit to hold it tight.

It just takes some changes in your life and your lifestyle.

The problem with most people is that they resist change. They don't really see a real need for change which makes it even more difficult. There are two important steps you must take in order to ignite your passion to make changes:

1. Recognize that there is a problem that can be improved by change.

2. Identify the obstacles and challenges that keep you from making changes.

Once you do these two things, it becomes much easier to see how change can make a tremendous improvement in your life. That first step is critical and it is always the hardest step to take.

Why? Because people find themselves saying:

- "I'm just a little overweight"

- "My life is pretty happy as it is"

- "I'm just a little in debt"

- "I ONLY have $6,000 in debt on my credit cards"

- "I'll make bigger payments next month"

- "I'll worry about investing and retirement when the children are older"

- "I deserve to buy nice things on credit because I work hard"

- "Once I have all the things I want, I can focus on my mental and spiritual growth"

Do you see yourself in any of these scenarios or similar ones? It's hard to take steps to make change when you don't even realize you need to do it. You can see how denial is your biggest enemy! Recognition of the problem and admitting that you need to make changes is the first vital step.

People resist change. They are not willing to accept the challenges that go with making changes. And many people worry that they will not be successful at making changes – demonstrating failure instead. But when you recognize that change is truly needed, you've overcome the hardest part of the process.

Once you make the decision to make changes, the next step is challenging but it comes much easier. There are many obstacles which you perceive will preclude you from making changes and reaching your goals:

- "My job is secure and I'm afraid to risk it"
- "I'm dependent on the money I make"
- "My wife/husband would not be supportive of a change"
- "My children are depending on me and I have to ensure stability"
- "I don't have the training or education to change careers"
- "If I start saving money for emergencies or retirement, I won't have enough to buy daily essentials"

- "I might fail and people will laugh at me"

The list can go on and on. People perceive they have more obstacles than they usually do. Many of the 'perceived' obstacles are actually not obstacles at all! For example, one man was concerned that his wife would not support changes in his job and down-sizing their lifestyle to pay off debt and live simpler. When he cautiously approached her, she broke down in tears.

Why?

She was so happy that he was ready to make changes for them all to live a better life and free themselves from the debt and stress of their current life, she couldn't believe it. She was excited about the wonderful new possibilities of living a simply happy and debt-free life!

A major 'obstacle' resolved!

Simply living

Simply living is about living a happy, fulfilled life that has purpose and meaning. It's about having control over how and where you spend your money, and how you spend your time. When you establish goals for a satisfying life, you take control of the present and the future and you will quickly learn that 'less is more'.

In a world where hyperconsumerism is rampant, you can bask in the glow of a newfound freedom from debt. But it's not just being debt-free that helps you create the life you desire. It involves more than money. You focus not only on your financial wealth, but you create a new life that encompasses:

1. Financial wealth

2. Mental wealth

3. Physical wealth

4. Spiritual wealth

Simply living gives you fulfillment and joy in living every day. It doesn't take money to be happy, but you may find that being happy leads to more meaningful jobs and work that can result in having more money. When you are happier with your work, your life, your family, and yourself, you are more productive and creative.

You identify new ways to build wealth in all areas of your life. The focus is no longer on the material possessions of the world or the social clout you have. It's about a life lived to its fullest – with purpose and meaning.

In this book, we'll open your eyes to a whole new world of pleasure and enjoyment and help you learn how to escape the bondage of consumerism and debt. In the process, you'll learn how to enjoy the simple things in life, nurture your mental capacities, and cultivate your spiritual self for a happier, more fulfilled life.

And all by living simply happy and debt-free!

Life is a balancing act

Today's hectic world requires multi-tasking at every level. Work, family, and social life are all filled with numerous activities and demands on our time. It's difficult to determine where and how to spend your time with so many commitments and activities tugging at you. It's a balancing act that feels more like a juggling act and it has most people filled with anxiety and stress.

Over 70% of Americans live paycheck to paycheck, with no cushion or planning for emergencies. They are juggling their money and their debt and getting nowhere – except further in debt and perilously close to a mental breakdown from the stress and anxiety of their situation. Their lives are so stressful and difficult, they don't have time to enjoy living.

But when you make the commitment to simplify your life and live a good life while still taking care of every other aspect of your life, it becomes a much more manageable task. It all starts with a good hard look at what's important to you in this life. It requires you to:

1. Clearly understand your personal situation

2. Recognize your issues

3. Identify what keeps you from reaching your goals

4. Determine what capabilities you have to succeed

5. Develop a plan for change

Insightful thinking and honestly answering questions about your current life, compared to the life you would really like to live, will lead to a greater understanding of what is needed to achieve that new life. Pulling back the covers and accepting the cold, hard facts about what is wrong with your current life will eventually lead to a better life.

You must take control of your life and make changes to reach the destination you dream about. Don't just think about it – take action and take control of your life. When you are in control, you are able to overcome obstacles and identify capabilities deep inside you that until now, you did not know existed.

It's an enlightening, exciting realization to discover that you can control your own destiny!

Consider some of the questions that will give you a greater understanding of your current situation and the simpler life that that awaits you:

- What gives you pleasure and makes you happy?
- Where are you spending your time?
- Where do you want to spend your time?
- What are your goals?
- What are your values and are they aligned with your goals?
- What are your priorities in life?
- Are you spending your time on the right things to achieve your goals?
- Where do your family and friends fit in with your goals?
- What's keeping you from achieving your goals?
- What's keeping you from living the life you've always wanted to live?
- How can you overcome the obstacles?
- What can you change?

- What capabilities, talents, and skills do you bring to the table?
- How can you leverage your abilities better to attain the life you desire?

Looking at yourself honestly and assessing your current situation is a harsh reality for many. Once you sit down and evaluate where you are currently spending your time, money, and energy, you may be surprised at the choices you have made. You may discover that your actions are not aligned with your goals.

And more importantly, you may realize that your goals are in conflict with your values!

Scary?

It can be, but it doesn't have to be.

Change can be hard and it may be painful – but the pain will be short-lived and your new life will be abundant with happiness. If you don't change, aren't you going to go through even more pain with no end to your debt, unhappiness, and stress in sight?

Goals, values, and priorities

Simplifying your life starts with clarifying your short and long term goals, and establishing your priorities. It means making decisions about how you'll spend your money, your time, your energy, and your efforts. Learning that the things that mean the most to you are the things you neglect the most in life is a real awakening for many people.

That's why we talk so much about the importance of recognizing your situation and admitting there is a problem. It takes determination and hard work to make change, but change is what creates a better life and a better way of doing things.

Take control

For many people, only a life-changing or catastrophic event can ignite the passion and fire within them. It's unfortunate that so many people travel aimlessly through life because they haven't taken time to align their values and their goals. They aren't willing to make changes until they are forced to make them because of an occurrence in their lives.

Wouldn't you rather have control over your own situation rather than wait for debt-collectors to knock on your door, or find your job is being eliminated and you have no savings to fall back on, or having a heart attack because you're overweight and unhealthy?

Alignment of the vital components of your life will help you to identify the life you truly want to live. They will help you to live simply and live debt-free with the right kind of planning and foresight.

Consider the 'rat race' that many people live in their daily lives. They spend more time at work to make more money for more things. It has become an obsession to spend money and show others how 'wealthy' they are.

People believe that 'things' give them the opportunity to live the good life. But what they fail to realize is that they don't have time to enjoy life and take advantage of the fruits of their labor when they are so focused on a hectic, unfocused life.

They are so busy making a living that they forget to live. And on top of it all, they are still in debt! The big houses, cars, vacations, and other entrapments have stolen life from them. The very thing they sought to create has robbed them of simply living the life they savor.

Their life is totally out of control. But they can regain control!

Assessing your own life

The first step in being simply happy and debt-free is to determine where you are in your pursuit of life today. Once you recognize the need to make changes, you can begin the process of assessing and evaluating your current situation.

These two examples will help clarify how you can better assess your own values, goals, and priorities.

1. Imagine your goals are:

    a. having the biggest house in the most prestigious neighborhood of the city

    b. owning the newest, sleekest model of car imaginable

    c. having a huge array of material possessions to showcase your success

d. making lots of money or using
      credit cards to acquire these
      possessions

Your values are:

   a. material possessions

   b. money

   c. prestige

   d. personal recognition

   e. elevated social status

Your priorities are based on spending fortunes, and stockpiling your possessions, at the cost of ignoring the other aspects of your life.

You are totally immersed in achieving your goals based on your values, and you have prioritized your life to attain them. You are even going as far as to maximize your credit cards and take on additional debt to buy the things you desire. You are sacrificing quality time with your family and neglecting your own personal mental and physical health.

Now imagine your goals are:

    a. providing for the things your family needs

    b. being debt-free and financially independent

    c. spending quality time with family and friends

    d. taking care of your own personal and spiritual needs

Your values are:

    a. family

    b. independence

    c. peace and tranquility

    d. financial health

    e. high quality of life personally and spiritually

Your goals and priorities are based on making a living at a job where you can produce a comfortable income, investing your money wisely for financial independence, affording time for family and friends, and allowing time for exercising, meditating, or other activities to enrich your personal and spiritual life.

In the two examples above, the goals, values, and priorities are well-aligned. Although you may not agree with one scenario or the other, you can see that each person is focusing on the things that are important to them.

Now, imagine your goals and values are related to #2 above, and your priorities are based on #1. This means you are working an exorbitant amount of time to make massive amounts of money to buy lots of material possessions - and you are even going into serious debt to make it happen too.

- You have abandoned your own personal goals and values to live a life that is fraught with stress, anxiety, and distress.

- Your goals, values, and priorities are totally out of alignment.

- You are madly working toward goals that are in total conflict with the things you hold near and dear to your heart and your life.

- You have sacrificed the life you desire for the life you have.

- You are living someone else's life!

Based on the life you are living in this scenario:

> Are you happy? No.

> Is this the life you want to live? No.

> Is it the life you are living? Yes.

> Does it have to be this way? No.

> Can you change and redirect your life? Absolutely!

> Can you overcome obstacles to get there? Definitely!

If you are interested in being simply happy and debt-free, then it's time for you to examine your current situation and create the life you desire. It's time for you to make changes that will lead to happiness and a better quality of life.

Standing up for yourself and what you value in life is now your mantra and your passion! You CAN make it happen.

Values

Beginning the process of living simply happy and debt-free requires that you identify your values. Keep in mind that values are the things you strive for in life and they should be a beacon of light to you in everything you do. Your values shine before you and light your path to reach your goals.

Learning to be simply happy means knowing exactly what is important to you in life.

It's not about things – it's about beliefs and principles.

Once you identify your values, it is much easier to establish your goals. As you define your values, think about what you want to do. Maybe independence, security, and spirituality are important to you. Perhaps power, authority, and adventure are your values.

Be honest with yourself and clarify your values. Once you recognize your values:

✓ assess how your goals and actions in life align with your values

✓ determine if you are effectively prioritizing your actions

✓ determine if you are living the life you want to live based on your values

✓ think about things in your life that take you further away from your values

✓ consider any hindrances that prohibit you from living your life based on your personal values.

Now that your values are crystal clear to you, begin living your life today based on your values. Keep them firmly in your mind and stay focused on your values as you determine your goals. Let your values direct your path and your actions towards a better life.

Goals

Many people never take time to truly establish goals for their lives. They either don't see the point or they don't believe it's important. Some people don't know what they want out of life while others are afraid to set goals for fear of not achieving them. And some people don't even know how to begin setting goals because they've never given it much thought.

But setting goals is what provides you with the roadmap to achieving the things that are important to you. Establishing a goal drives you to a destination. And reaching your destination helps you establish new goals. It's a lifelong process of deciding where you want to go, creating plans to get there, and establishing new goals once you arrive.

Reaching your goals is a fulfilling and satisfying experience. It gives you confidence and motivation to move forward. It also gives you the satisfaction of knowing that you have accomplished an important milestone in your life while holding true to your personal values.

What could be more rewarding!

Four aspects of life

There are four (4) primary capacities of life that create a healthy balance for a happier life. These four areas are all interrelated and interconnected through your core values and beliefs. How you approach them is based on how you view life and what you believe is important.

The four aspects of life are:

1. Financial wealth

2. Physical wealth

3. Mental wealth

4. Spiritual wealth

Maybe you've never considered these things as part of your 'wealth'. But when you are financially independent, physically fit, mentally well, and spiritually grounded, then you are certainly wealthy in all aspects! Your values enable you to achieve high levels of satisfaction in all areas of your life when you stay true to them as your guiding light.

Understanding how each capacity of your life contributes to the others, and achieving a healthy level of wealth in each one, will lead you to a live a life that is simply happy and debt-free.

Open your mind, your heart, and your senses to a new way of life as we explore further. Learning the steps to achieving wealth in all areas of your life will be a life-altering experience.

Financial wealth and independence

Much has been written about financial freedom and independence. But it seems that it is still difficult for people to really grasp what that means. People associate wealth with riches and they erroneously assume that financial freedom means having money to buy anything they want.

According to Webster's dictionary, 'wealth' is defined as:

> ❖ people who have an abundance of material possessions.

It does not say:

> ❖ "people who have an abundance of material possessions *that are paid for*"!

So, what's the difference?

Having a lot of material possessions may also equate to having a lot of debt. As a matter of fact, many people who live a high-consumption lifestyle actually have little money, few investments, and no appreciable assets. They have made it a priority to garner more material possessions than to establish financial independence. Their desire for immediate gratification leaves them with no emergency fund, no retirement planning, and a great deal of mental and physical stress.

The staggering debt that is amassed by many people leads to chronic stress and anxiety. The mental burden of handling this stress often results in physical ailments and poor health. Their inability to control their lives and their expenses has driven them to a point where they see no way out. Being in the jaws of debt can create an unhappy, unhealthy living environment.

But, there is a way out. It all comes down to values, goals, and priorities. Once you are able to clarify these things, you are ready to begin your plan for living simply happy.

Steps to financial independence

There are some key steps and major milestones that will help you achieve the financial independence you desire and become debt-free. It takes discipline, commitment, and planning. Taking the time and effort to achieve a debt-free status will energize you to do the things you want to do for a happier and more fulfilled life.

The major steps involved with preparing for financial independence include:

1. Pay yourself first.
2. Prepare for emergencies.
3. Pay off existing debt.
4. Plan for a 3-6 month crisis.
5. Prepare for college expenses early.
6. Build wealth by investing.

We'll examine each of these steps in detail as we establish a long-term plan for your financial happiness. Approaching this process with a mental attitude that focuses positively on the process and looks forward to the outcome will make it much easier to achieve.

It will take some time – but remember that you didn't get where you are today overnight.

It's like gaining weight. You may think you're a "little overweight". But you don't do anything about it. You wake up one day and you're suddenly 20, 30, or 40 pounds overweight!

How did it happen? It happened one pound at a time.

And debt happens one purchase at a time!

Pay yourself first

When considering the many ways you can manage your finances, it's an important rule to always pay yourself first. This means having money deducted from your paycheck to cover your retirement and future financial planning. When money is automatically deducted from your check, you are not tempted to use it for other non-essentials.

Most employers also offer some type of matching program for people who save for the future. They may match 50% or 100% of what you save up to a certain percentage. You should always take advantage of these situations to the greatest extent possible. If you don't, it's like leaving money on the table!

Taking advantage of any type of employer matching plan for any type of savings such as a 401K retirement plan is one of the smartest things you can do.

For example:

- if your employer offers to match everything you save up to a maximum of 4%, 5%, or more, then you immediately double your money up to that maximum. In this example, if you save $50 per month, your employer matches it $50, then you now have $100 saved per month.

Nowhere else will you make this kind of return on your money. In addition to the match from your employer, you are also allowing your savings to grow through investing. There is absolutely no reason or excuse not to participate in this type of employer matching plan!

You don't believe you can do this because you are already in debt and can't pay your credit cards? Think again.

Part of being financially independent means preparing for your future. Starting with a small amount in a savings plan that is matched by your employer will get you to financial independence faster than you could ever do alone. Once you are debt-free, you can increase the amount of money you are saving to optimize the employer match.

And even if your employer does not have a matching plan, you can't afford not to prepare for your future. Putting money into a 401K retirement plan or similar savings is tax-deferred money that helps reduce the money you pay in taxes today. It's a win-win situation for you.

Once you have become debt-free, the amount you contribute to this type of plan may increase. But for now, start putting some money towards your future and focus on realizing your goal of becoming debt-free.

Paying yourself first is an important rule that all 'millionaires' subscribe to. They know the critical importance of investing and saving for the future. They are less likely to focus on instant gratification than the average person – and that's how many of them became millionaires.

Slow, methodical investing and watching their money work for them is their secret and it can be yours too. It just takes commitment and discipline.

Prepare for emergencies

Things change and sometimes an expense may come out of the blue. Being prepared for these types of expenses is essential. A good way to prepare for this is to put a small amount of money in a checking or savings account that is used ONLY for emergencies.

For example, discovering that you need a new set of tires for your car can be disastrous if you're not prepared. You may need to replace a worn-out heating unit in your house. An emergency fund helps you handle this type of emergency without the stress and anxiety of being surprised.

You need to decide what is comfortable for you based on your personal situation. But at a minimum, you should consider building an emergency fund of at least $1,000 for now.

Having an emergency fund enables you to handle urgent situations without having to resort to using credit cards. You are working hard to become debt-free and one emergency can sabotage your efforts if you don't handle it carefully. Being prepared for the unexpected is one of your best defense mechanisms.

Even if you only have $10 each month to contribute to this emergency fund, do it! Before you know it, you'll have a nice emergency fund established and greater peace of mind.

Pay off existing debt

Credit card debt is one of your primary stressors and paying it off should be one of your key goals. This is the quickest way to financial independence. Creating a plan to pay off credit cards is essential. It starts by slowly reducing the debt and then eventually eliminating it altogether.

Did you know that over 80% of college students finish school with some credit card debt? That means that most people starting out in their working life will start with debt. Unfortunately, many people just allow it to snowball from that point and credit cards become a way of life. This is especially true for people who demand instant gratification and subscribe to the "I've got to have it now" theory of life.

The first step to becoming debt-free is to avoid accumulating further debt. Don't continue to use your credit cards while trying to eliminate the debt! You'll certainly fail. It's best to destroy all credit cards except one major card with the lowest interest rate.

Avoid the temptation to keep all of your cards in your wallet where they can be easily accessed and quickly 'swiped' through the cash register to add even more debt. Keeping that ONE card for emergency expenses or other critical purchases will be enough.

The following steps will help you whittle your credit card debt down to zero. But remember that it does take commitment, determination, and persistence for this to work. We never said it would be easy.

But it is possible and well worthwhile!

1. If possible, consolidate your credit cards onto the single card with the lowest monthly interest rate. Contact the credit card company and let them know that you plan to consolidate all debt on one card and request a lower interest rate. They may be willing to give you a lower rate to retain your business and move all other balances to this one card.

2. If you are unable to consolidate your debt onto one card for some reason, then focus on paying the card with the highest interest rate first. Paying a high rate of interest can easily have you paying $1,500 or more for a $1,000 purchase! Imagine the accumulation of debt when you pay so much more for the things you buy.

3. Pay as much towards the credit card debt as you are able to pay each month. Strive to consistently pay more than the minimum. Otherwise, you are giving your money away and paying hundreds of dollars in interest and fees – digging your debt deeper with every payment! Stretch your money as far as you can and pay as much as possible towards credit card debt each month.

   If this means eliminating expenses elsewhere in your budget to make a higher credit card payment, then by all means do it. If you routinely eat out for lunch or dinner, then change your habits and prepare a lower cost meal at home or take your lunch to work.
   Eliminate the $5 mocha latté from your daily routine. Carpool to work with a friend. Find ways to reduce expenses in other areas and apply the savings toward credit card payments. The faster you can pay off credit card debt, the sooner you'll be financially independent.

4. Once your credit card debt is paid off, congratulate yourself on accomplishing this goal! You've done a great job of managing your money and staying true to your values by focusing on your goal.

You're now one step closer to financial independence and being simply happy.

5. Now that your credit card debt is eliminated, apply the money previously used for paying off the cards to your future security. Do not be tempted to start 'spending' this extra money and do NOT be tempted to begin using credit cards again!

   Increase the amount you withhold from your paycheck to 'pay yourself first' and build your 401K savings faster now that you don't have to pay towards credit card debt. And, increase the amount you put into your emergency fund. It's time to start accumulating wealth!

You may be asking how you can find the money to pay off credit cards and still pay for your day to day living expenses. It is a challenging situation and we never said this would be easy. You got into this situation one purchase at a time. Now you'll have to get out of it one credit card payment at a time.

But it CAN be done!

Examining your current lifestyle and how you spend your money will help. If you're really serious about making changes and being simply happy and debt-free, then this might include downsizing to a smaller house, or trading for a more economical car. Maybe it means foregoing those expensive dinners out and cooking in instead.

It all depends on your situation, your level of debt, and how much change you are willing to make to live the life you desire.

Some ideas you should consider include:

> As mentioned earlier, is the house you live in the house you want to live in? Or is it "show" others you have money? If downsizing is an option, now is the time to consider it. This is a critical decision as you evaluate your values and goals. It's an important part of your planning to become debt-free and financially independent.

> Do you have luxury cars that can be traded for more economical versions? Will this help with any existing car debt?

> Eating out is expensive – evaluate how much you spend eating out and find ways to trim expenses from this budget by cooking at home, taking your lunch to work, or other small changes. These small

changes can add up to big bucks over time. Isn't that how you got into this situation anyway – a lot of small charges accumulating over time to become an enormous debt burden?

➢ Being a member of a country club, pool, or other social group may be important to you. But if it's not and you're serious about being debt-free, consider cancelling your membership. Are there are social opportunities, activities, and things you can do that are free or lower cost and still fulfill your needs?

➢ Determine where your money goes each month related to purchases such as clothes, shoes, home furnishings, and other material items. Can they be eliminated or reduced? Do you really need those new shoes? Are expensive designer clothes worth the difference in money to you?

➢ Consider money spent on lawn or garden care. Is that something you can eliminate and take care of those things yourself or manage by engaging other family members to help?

➢ Is it possible to carpool to work to save gas?

➢ Some people pay for every bell and whistle offered with their cable television but they hardly ever use the premium channels and other services. Make sure this is money you truly want to spend and if not, make changes!

➢ Evaluate your cell phone bills and make sure you have the best plan possible for your situation. If you're constantly going over your 'minutes allowance' and paying $.40 per minute for those extra minutes, consider a new plan – OR, reduce your phone usage! Find a way to cut these costs.

➢ If you have a housekeeper or other domestic help, consider having the family take on much of this responsibility and eliminate this expense from your budget.

There are literally dozens of ways to reduce or eliminate expenses. Just be creative, stay true to your values, and make changes to meet your goals! You'll find that you don't even miss most of the things you eliminate from your life. You'll also find that your life becomes richer when you focus on the simple things that are important to you.

Plan for a 3-6 month crisis

Life happens and we never know what we may be faced with. We talked about a small emergency fund earlier, but once you are able to get your debt under control, it's time to talk about a more extensive savings plan. All financial planners recommend at least 3-6 months worth of savings to cover expenses in case you are laid off from your job, become ill, or you have to face some other situation which temporarily affects your income.

Economic downturns, job layoffs, illness, family crisis, and many other things can throw a kink into the best-laid plans. Having a savings account that will cover 3-6 months worth of expenses is essential as you begin to focus on financial independence. This will give you incredible peace of mind too.

Money that was previously used for credit card payments can be applied to this savings. Focus on building this account as quickly as possible. Manage expenses and eliminate unnecessary expenditures each month. Apply the savings to this account and create a healthy financial cushion in the event that the unexpected happens.

When you're prepared for the worst, you'll have a lot less stress and worry about what 'might happen'. You may never need to use this savings, but the peace of mind and independence you feel by having it will be a tremendous reward for your efforts.

Being truly debt-free also means being financially independent. A savings account that will cover 3-6 months of general expenses is an important part of your overall independence. If you never have to use it – that's great! It can continue to help you build your financial wealth as your money works for you by accumulating interest.

Prepare for college expenses

Being prepared for the expenses resulting from college tuition for children can be daunting to the wealthiest person. But it is a reality that most children will have a desire to attend some type of college today, and it is important to prepare for this situation. Even if you are only able to put a small amount of money into a college savings account monthly, it is worth the effort.

You can establish a personal savings account for this purpose or participate in a State savings plan such as a 529 Plan. State savings plans offer great opportunities to save for college that will result in lower costs when it's time for your child to attend. It's worth looking into these plans and the benefits they offer.

When the time comes that your child(ren) are ready for college, you'll be glad you made this investment in their future. It will be a relief to you as you watch the fund grow and the reward to both you and your child(ren) will be great. It will give you a good sense of independence to know that you are taking this important step for the future of your children.

Remember that over 80% of children graduate from college with some credit card debt. Not only are you able to help with tuition payments, but you are teaching your children a lesson about financial planning and looking to the future without using credit cards. It's a valuable lesson that will benefit them for years to come.

Build wealth by investing

Now it's time to get serious about financial independence and building wealth. You've worked hard for your money – now it's time for your money to work hard for you. Most people don't even realize that when their money works for them, they can become wealthier quicker than if they were working harder themselves!

Investing money in addition to your 401K, Roth IRA, or other long-term savings plans is essential for long-term financial wealth and independence. These types of plans, especially when there is an employer match, will help you to build your financial wealth steadily, but other types of investment plans are also available to you.

Mutual fund families such as Vanguard, T. Rowe Price, and others are good options to consider. Contact them directly and they'll help you create a plan that will put you on the road to building wealth. Money market funds are a great place to invest your money and they also offer easy access if you need to withdraw funds.

You can also engage a financial advisor, certified financial planner (CFP) or certified public accountant (CPA) to help with managing your financial portfolio, but be careful of management fees and commissions you'll pay for their services. Search for a 'fee only' consultant to optimize your return on investment. Make sure you understand how services are reimbursed and what that will cost you in the long-term.

Bottom line is to invest your money where the return is good and your investments contribute to your sense of well-being and future financial security.

Let your money work for you!

And remember – STAY debt-free. Getting to this point is only the beginning. You must work hard and stay focused on your goals in order to stay debt-free. Don't allow yourself to slip into the habit of using your credit cards again, except in emergencies. If you can't pay off your entire credit card bill in one month, then don't charge on it!

Absolutely do NOT be tempted to dip into your savings, 401K, and other investments. Allow them to grow and provide the financial security and wealth you desire. Remember that most plans have a high penalty for early withdrawal of funds and this can negate all of the hard work you have put into your financial planning so far.

When you live below your means as we have discussed earlier, you are able to live comfortably and happily without disrupting your long-term savings plans. Living below your means will never require you to utilize your credit cards again either.

It's that simple – staying out of debt is much easier than climbing out of the deep hole of debt!

It doesn't take a millionaire to live simply happy. But living simply happy can result in your becoming wealthy if you live below your means and invest wisely. Always enjoy life, stay true to your values, and follow your goals while your money works for you.

You've succeeded in financial wealth!

Your financial health is in excellent condition – you've succeeded and you should be proud of your accomplishments! Credit card debt is now history and you're on your way to financial independence!

Now it's important to stay focused on your goals and stay true to your values. Attaining a position of good financial health is just one part of your strategy toward being simply happy. This is when you really start building financial wealth and begin truly focusing on the other aspects of your life.

Just like you invest time in your financial future, you must invest in your mental, physical, and spiritual future as well.

Athletes don't simply decide to run a marathon. They don't just decide to participate in the Olympics. They set goals, practice, practice more, and become excellent runners, or skaters, or gymnasts.

People don't suddenly decide to become yoga masters and are immediately able to focus their minds for inner peace and spiritual enlightenment. They set a goal, study, practice, meditate, and practice more until they attain higher levels of achievement and become masters.

It's the same way with your life. You are rewarded for the time and effort you invest in all areas of your life. The more passionate you are and the better you prepare for your future, the happier your life will be.

Now, it's time to focus more fully on your mental, physical, and spiritual health and wealth. The sooner you get them in excellent condition, the sooner you can enjoy the life you were meant to live.

When you have achieved financial independence and are on the road to financial wealth, you are able to live your life more fully. You can enjoy the simple things in life and dedicate more time to your family, friends, and yourself.

Who is really wealthy?

People who are perceived to have lots of money may not be the people you think they are. They're probably not the people living in the 'right' neighborhoods and showcasing volumes of material possessions - because they probably have mounds of credit card debt.

Instead, you'll find that the truly wealthy people are those who don't outwardly appear to be 'wealthy' in the strictest sense of the word. Consider how the following people may actually be the wealthiest.

- The man next door may be a millionaire.

- The woman you see using coupons in the grocery market may be wealthy.

- The guy you see playing with his kids in the park may be wealthy.

- The small shop owner down the street may be a millionaire.

Millionaires and wealthy people don't usually drive the big fancy cars, or live in the opulent homes, and wear the designer fashions of the day. They actually live well below their means and their prudent lifestyle is often what made them wealthy. They don't worry about impressing their neighbors and friends with flashy materialism, but they prefer to enjoy the finer things in life such as time shared with friends and family.

To them, the finer things in life are friends, family, health, spirituality, and love. They manage their money and their time in a way that enables them to remain independent and simply happy. "Quiet millionaires" don't concern themselves with social status and the trappings of high society life.

Appearances can be deceiving and the truly independent, wealthy, happy people know this for a fact. Consumerism and over-spending is for those who have little money. Plastic cards can give the appearance of wealth to anyone. But to truly be wealthy means living a life that is simple, yet fulfilling and satisfying.

That means satisfying mentally, physically, and spiritually. To truly be wealthy, you must be able to enjoy these very important aspects of your life to their fullest.

When you are able to do this, then you will have attained real wealth!

Mental Wealth

Now that you've successfully managed to become debt-free, it's time to really start simply living and enjoying life to its fullest. A healthy mental attitude will be an important asset in keeping you focused on your values and your goals. It will help you remain debt-free and live a simpler life filled with things that bring enjoyment to you.

Financial independence puts you in control. You decide how to spend your money and your time. You can make choices that are based on your values and how you want to spend your life.

Consider the factors that contribute to your mental health in addition to the stress of financial issues. There are many factors that create a mental attitude of stress, anxiety, and even depression. These factors can impact the quality of life you live and can negatively impact your physical health as well.

Mental wealth comes from inside

Mental wealth comes from within you. It is not from working hard, stockpiling lots of possessions, or inheriting money. It comes from you and your own state of mind. Living life to the fullest means having financial freedom AND mental freedom, which equates to mental wealth.

Identifying the things that lead to mental wealth is the first step in your quest. Mental wealth starts with positive thinking and persistence. It requires thoughtful review of your current situation and how it affects your mental health.

Think about the things you do in your daily life and identify any areas of your life that create mental stress and fatigue.

For example:

❖ Do you enjoy your work and your job? Or does it cause your stress?

❖ Do you have a happy family situation that allows you to spend time with your family that you desire?

❖ Do you have enough time with your family?

❖ Are you choosing to do the things that bring you fulfillment and pleasure?

❖ Are you disciplined in staying true to your values in your everyday life – not just in your financial situation?

Many people think that once they are debt-free, they will lead a happier, more fulfilled life. But it takes more than just being debt-free. It takes being mentally and emotionally free too.

Goals and values align

When you align your values and your goals, your mental wealth will appreciate in value too. If your values are recognition and prestige for being financially wealthy, but you have set goals to live debt-free and simply, then something is wrong. You will never be mentally or emotionally happy because your values and goals are in conflict.

Your mental wealth is dependent on your ability to create goals that fulfill your values. Some potential values include:

1. Job security
2. Helping other people
3. Stability
4. Recognition
5. Status
6. Prestige
7. Job tranquility
8. Power and authority
9. Having and spending time with family
10. Friendships and strong relationships
11. Money
12. Time freedom

There are many values from which to choose, and you have to evaluate yourself honestly to identify your most important values. Your goals should be driven by your values.

Notice that job security and job tranquility are both listed above. To one person, it may be important to stay in a job that they don't really enjoy just because they know it is a secure job. But to another person, if they do not receive pleasure and tranquility from their job, their goal would be to change jobs because job tranquility overrides job security.

With this in mind, let's explore some of the daily activities of your life that affect your mental health and wealth. Understanding what contributes to a healthy mental status will enable you to better enjoy life and focus on the things that bring the most pleasure to you.

Job stress robs mental wealth

Unless they've inherited large sums of money and are independently wealthy, most people have to work at some type of job to make money for basic essentials and things they desire in life. Whether you have a high school education, college education, advanced degree, certification, or trade-school training, there is still a job for you somewhere.

People make decisions about education and jobs based on influences in their early lives. For example, your parents may think it is extremely important for you to attend a major university and become a lawyer, accountant, or doctor. They may influence you by talking about this and pushing you in that direction your entire life. They push their expectations on you and soon, these expectations become 'your goals'.

Parents usually want a better life for their children than they perceive they have for themselves. That's why they try to influence their children one way or the other. In their view, a college education that leads to one of the more 'prestigious' professions will bring you money, wealth, and happiness. In some cases that may be true.

But that is not always the case.

What if you realize that you don't enjoy the type of work you are doing? You've completed your college education, obtained your medical degree, and started a career as a doctor. You don't find the work fulfilling and you spend more hours working than you feel you should. The time you have left for your family and personal life is minimal and you are stressed.

At the same time, you are making a great salary with excellent benefits, but you're still not able to afford everything. You've resorted to using credit cards for many purchases and created a great debt chasm.

But you keep doing what you're doing 'for the sake of the family'.

How does this affect your mental health?

Most likely you are not happy with what you are doing. You may have an entrepreneurial spirit that is being slowly extinguished because you have gotten caught up in the trappings of an affluent, 'wealthy' lifestyle. Your salary pays some of the bills and the others are covered by credit card debt. You believe you will never be able to do what you love – at least not until you retire which could be in 40 more years!

That's a sad way to live for 30-40 years – **waiting** to do what you want to do! Waiting to live the life you want to live. Waiting to be happy.

A 2000 study, "Attitudes In the American Workplace VI"[2] found that:

- 80% of workers feel stress on the job

- 14% feel like striking a coworker

- 25% have felt like screaming or shouting due to job stress

A prior study by NIOSH[2] reported that:

- 25% of respondents view their jobs as the number one stressor in their lives

- 26% were 'often or very often burned out or stressed by their work'

- Confirmed job stress is more strongly associated with health complaints than financial or family problems

---

[2] http://www.stress.org/job.htm

Stress on the job is having a major impact on people's ability to manage their lives! The mental toll it is taking on them is creating a crisis for thousands of people. Yet they keep on doing what they are doing.

You see what stress and a poor mental outlook can do to you. Now, step back and determine what obstacles are in your way of doing what you really want to do. You know that your salary is a key driver for why you spend your time at a job you dislike. But is it possible to do something you love and live on less money?

Is less more?

Consider the possibilities of exploring what you love to do and creating a plan to reach that goal. After all, half of the battle to making change is making a mental commitment to do so.

A case study

A case study may help you see that there are ways to overcome the mental and emotional blackmail that is inflicted on many people who believe they are 'stuck' in their jobs.

"My parents pushed me for years to prepare for college and become a lawyer. They saw this as a way for me to reach high levels of wealth, recognition, and prestige. They truly believed it would lead me to a happy life that would be filled with great material possessions and financial security. I was greatly influenced by them throughout my high school years and continued my education to please them – soon becoming a graduate of a highly esteemed university and joining a prestigious law firm. I never stopped to think about doing anything else.

I focused on my career for years, putting in long hours and working extremely hard to build my career. My wife and I married after two years of dating and soon had two beautiful children. To everyone else, we appeared to have all of the material things we wanted – a magnificent house in the 'right' neighborhood, great cars, designer clothes, membership to the country club, and many of the other amenities that accompany this 'rich' lifestyle.

But neither my wife nor I were truly happy and we certainly weren't wealthy. It only appeared that we were 'wealthy. Far from it. Our lavish lifestyle had taken its toll on me financially, mentally, and physically. I had maxed out our credit cards, was paying a mortgage that was outrageous, and was participating in events and activities that took me away from my family – just to stay involved in the 'right' social circles and maintain a social standing in the community. I was working at a demanding job just to keep our heads above water and I dreaded walking into the office every day.

And on top of it all, I was spending an inordinate amount of time at the office to accumulate billable hours. Why? To afford the lifestyle we were living – and that we didn't even enjoy! That's when I realized that my mental health was suffering and so was the mental and emotional health of my family. But I saw no way out.

Until one day, with the help of my wife, I sat down and created a plan to make a difference. I had to be brutally honest with myself and my wife was critical to the process. We both looked at what we had accumulated – including DEBT – and proceeded to create a list of things that were important to us.

The list turned out to be our values even though we didn't realize it at the time. It included strong family relationships, good physical health, financial independence, creativity, free time, and spiritual strength.

What an eye-opener!

*Our **goals** were focused on values more related to prestige, recognition, power, authority, and wealth. We were living a 'fake life' that had totally misaligned values and goals. Our next step was to determine what obstacles stood in our way of our real values and dreams.*

As you can imagine, money was number one. We had become accustomed to the money I was making, and the use of credit cards to get the things we hadn't earned the money for yet. Disappointment from my parents was also on the list – and it was then that I realized that I was doing what I was doing for someone else. Facing potential embarrassment and rejection from my friends and associates fell on the list as well.

Once we had identified all of the obstacles and realized that each one could be overcome, we became excited about our future. We talked about spending more time together as a family. We talked about taking better care of ourselves.

Both of us had a strong interest and desire to open an antique store and the idea of it really happening was invigorating! It was something we had talked about for years and thought we might do when we retired. Everything we valued in life had been put on hold – but it didn't have to be! Our creativity came alive and our values overtook us as we created a plan for our future.

This was a plan that would have us living debt-free without the shackles of a demanding, high pressure corporate job. And it would also provide the opportunity to live true to our values of spending time with our family and taking care of ourselves. The awakening was incredible and our planning began in earnest.

It didn't happen overnight – it took persistence, patience, and commitment to our values and our goals. It took a lot of change. And it took determination. But we made it!

We down-sized our house to a more affordable one, kept one of our existing cars, and traded the other one for a more economical one. We chipped away at our credit card debt month after month and erased it completely. We quickly started putting money into our 401K account to prepare for the future we envisioned.

We found that we no longer needed the country club membership because we were too busy spending time with our family at State parks, nature trails, picnics, and scenic drives through the mountains.

.
But most of all, we were spending time managing our own antique business where we met new, interesting, and unique people almost every day! We shared stories about the antiques and we frequented antique shows and gatherings where people shared memories of times long ago and focused on things that brought happiness to them.

For the first time in my life, I was truly happy and satisfied. I was simply happy and debt-free and loving life! The investment I made in my mental wealth was reaping a huge return on my investment and I began to feel, look, and be simply happy! Financial independence lead to mental, physical, and spiritual wealth and independence too.

My wife and I spend more time together and our children are learning more about the world than about material possessions and the lives of the 'wealthy'.

Now, we are truly rich!

We continue to manage our antique business and enjoy watching it grow. We are financially independent and we also enjoy building our wealth and letting our money work for us. We're amazed at how quickly our money has grown while we've been enjoying the life we were meant to live. Making changes was not easy, but it was temporary and we are now happier than we've ever been before.

We may not have the income we once had or the trappings of a wealthy lifestyle, but we are definitely emotionally and mentally wealthy now! Our minds are clear and focused because we hold true to our values everyday.

It has made a difference in our lives that has given us the mental and physical capacity to enjoy every second of this life – simply happy and debt-free!"

This story may seem unbelievable to you, but it happens to a lot of people. Getting out of the rat-race and creating a life that is simple and happy is possible – no matter what your station in life. You may not even need to make the drastic changes that this family made, but simple changes can also make a huge difference in how you live your life.

But it does take a commitment to making changes and creating well-defined goals to guide you to your destination. Most people don't like change, but change is necessary if you want things to improve.

It takes positive thinking, determination, fortitude, and persistence to live the life you want to live – especially if you're already immersed in a career you don't enjoy and surrounded by piles of debt that you can't see beyond. It takes change to make a difference.

It's easy to see how the financial and mental aspects of your life are so entwined. Your belief system and values should be your driving force, and when they are not in synch with your daily living and the work you do, it's time to stop and think about what's important to you.

You don't have to be a doctor, a lawyer, or an executive to make this kind of change in your life. You may be a call center agent, a programmer, an administrative assistant, a bookkeeper, a real estate agent, or any number of occupations.

But if you're not happy doing what you're doing and you feel financially and emotionally trapped, then your mental health will suffer and you will never be mentally or financially wealthy.

But I love my job

The example above assumes you are in a job or occupation you don't like. However, you may perfectly happy with your work but you have just allowed your debt to overtake your happiness. You may not want to change jobs but something is just not right. When you overcome your debt, your job may become more fulfilling to you. The most important thing is to be happy with what you are doing and if you're not, examine the reasons why.

Once you recognize what is causing you to be mentally unhappy and fatigued, you can decide how to make changes to improve your mental health. Becoming debt-free is just part of the problem. Becoming mentally wealthy is a big part of your happiness and your success.

Consider how your job affects your mental wealth and if it is not a deterrent, then look at other aspects of your life. Whether it's the amount of time you spend with your family, the time you give back to others, or any other number of things, you can make changes to do what you really want to do in life. Once you become debt-free, you have more freedom to make choices and changes in your life so take advantage of this wonderful opportunity to live life simply happy.

Take time to evaluate your situation and decide if you need to make changes to increase your mental wealth:

1. Identify and write-down your values and be honest with yourself.

2. Establish the goals you want to achieve.

3. Identify the obstacles and challenges keeping you from achieving these goals.

4. Create solutions and ideas to overcome the challenges.

5. Create a plan to make changes and follow the plan.

6. Follow the steps in the "Financial Wealth" section of this book and start managing

and building your financial wealth while doing the things you love. You'll build financial wealth by living below your means, investing in your future, preparing for the unexpected, and letting your money work for you – just like many millionaires have done successfully!

7. Live a life that is mentally, emotionally, and financially 'wealthy' by staying true to your values and striving for your goals! Stay focused.

Anyone can achieve anything that they truly desire and believe they can accomplish.

You must have the confidence, desire, ambition, and persistence to achieve your goals. It won't happen overnight, but with planning, patience, and perseverance, you will succeed. It's all a matter of aligning your values and goals in a way that has you simply happy and living the life you always wanted to live.

The mind is a powerful thing – use it wisely and it will help you grow rich in many areas of your life – not only mentally but financially as well!

"If you fix your mind on the idea that your earning ability is limited, then indeed it is. You will never earn more than that self-set limit. The subconscious will create and maintain the limits you set."

Thomas D. Willhite from *The Book of Wealth*

Physical wealth

With your financial and mental wealth growing every day, it's important not to neglect your physical health either. Did you know that you can enjoy physical WEALTH too?

You take time to invest in your financial wealth and your financial future. You invest in your mental wealth. It's time to invest in your physical wealth and the future of your life. Goals which lead to a longer, happier life require that you are fit and able to enjoy that life.

The problem is big

It is estimated that the annual cost of obesity in America is $122.9 billion! Obesity and related conditions or diseases result in over $62 million in physician visits and over $40 million in missed time from work every year![3] In addition, obesity has been linked to diabetes, gallbladder disease, heart disease, and high blood pressure.

Obesity in America and in many other countries of the world has reached an all time high. There are many reasons for this:

1. People don't get the exercise they need

2. Fast food industries have made fat and sugar a staple in diets

3. Low cost of fast-food makes it attractive for young families

4. The rat-race lifestyle makes it harder for people to plan and prepare nutritious meals at home

---

[3] http://www.obesityinamerica.org/economicimpact.html

5. It's a "I gotta have it" world and that includes food

6. Mega and super-sized portions are packing on the weight

7. Mental and physical exhaustion are breaking down the resolve to eat nutritiously

There are many other reasons people don't eat nutritiously and exercise properly. It does take some planning and work to establish a good exercise routine and healthy eating habits. Financial, mental, and physical fitness are all important aspects of your life and they all contribute to living the life you want to live.

But you may not be overweight. You may just be a little sedentary in your lifestyle. Physical wealth is not just about weight. It's about anything that affects your body and your ability to enjoy life. Stress, anxiety, overweight, and living a sedentary lifestyle, have all contributed to illness or early death for many people.

How you invest your money determines how wealthy you will be in the future. The same principle applies to your body. How you take care of your body and invest time to be healthy determines whether or not you will be physically wealthy in years to come.

Building your retirement account requires commitment and persistence in saving small amounts of money. Eventually, it turns into millions of dollars when managed well and fed regularly.

Your body works the same way. Consistent amounts of exercise and a commitment to eating healthy will give you the body you need to enjoy life and be simply happy in everything you do. When you get moving, you'll feel better, your body will be in better shape, and your mental health will improve at the same time.

When you take care of yourself physically and live an active life, you contribute to your mental well-being and your ability to stay focused on your goals. Both physical and mental health help you stay focused on what is important to you. Your body is like a well-oiled machine where everything works in concert for optimal performance.

People often ignore their physical health while spending more time on other areas of their lives. But a simple investment in your physical health will bring you tremendous physical WEALTH! A healthy body is a happier body and you are able to achieve and accomplish more when you are physically fit.

The happiest people are those who are able to balance the work, family, and personal areas of their lives. They recognize the value and importance of managing their time wisely to allow for all aspects of their life to complement each other. Feeling good about yourself physically also contributes to a type of mental euphoria and that drives you to greater heights of success and well-being than you ever imagined.

Making changes requires a positive attitude

So, exactly how do you go about making changes in your physical health that will lead to physical wealth? It's very much like the changes you make in your financial and mental health.

It takes commitment, persistence, and determination. It starts with an examination of where you are today and where you want to be. It takes time to consider what is important to you and identifying how to get where you want to be. It requires you to establish goals.

But most of all, it takes a positive mental attitude and a *focus* on your goals. There are some milestones that will help you get started, similar to the mental wealth planning we've discussed above. Evaluating your current situation and comparing that with your desired goal gives you insightful information about whether or not you need to make changes.

Let's take a look at the evaluation and planning process:

1. Start by evaluating your current physical health situation. Look at your weight, level of fitness, cardio health, level of exercise, and other aspects of your physical health. Take a good honest look at how much time you currently invest in your physical health and make a note of it.

   Ask yourself some questions. Are you overweight? Do you tire easily? Can you climb two flights of stairs without becoming winded? Do you eat nutritiously? Do you know what foods are good for you and which ones are bad for your health? Do you have good heart health?

2. Now, compare where you are today to where you should be based on your own perceptions and based on health recommendations of your physician or other credible sources. You may not be

obese, but you may be a 'little overweight'. You may think you're a 'little sedentary'. Either way, there could be serious health consequences.

For example, you may be surprised at what you discover. Take a look at the Metropolitan Weight Table below, which is the 'gold standard' for weight management by most doctors and insurance plans. These recommended weights will help you assess your current level of fitness related to weight.

TABLE 1[4]
1999 METROPOLITAN HEIGHT AND WEIGHT TABLES
FOR
MEN AND WOMEN
According to Frame, Ages 25-59
WOMEN
Weight in Pounds (In Indoor Clothing)*

HEIGHT (In Shoes)+		SMALL FRAME	MEDIUM FRAME	LARGE FRAME
Feet	Inches			
4	10	102-111	109-121	118-131
4	11	103-113	111-123	120-134
5	0	104-115	113-126	122-137
5	1	106-118	115-129	125-140
5	2	108-121	118-132	128-143
5	3	111-124	121-135	131-147
5	4	114-127	124-138	134-151
5	5	117-130	127-141	137-155
5	6	120-133	130-144	140-159
5	7	123-136	133-147	143-163
5	8	126-139	136-150	146-167
5	9	129-142	139-153	149-170
5	10	132-145	142-156	152-173
5	11	135-148	145-159	155-176
6	0	138-151	148-162	158-179

[4] Source of basic data Build Study, 1979. Society of Actuaries and Association of Life Insurance Medical Directors of America, 1980. Copyright© 1996, 1999 Metropolitan Life Insurance Company. Courtesy of the Metropolitan Life Insurance Company.

- Indoor clothing weighing 5 pounds for men and 3 pounds for women.

+ Shoes with 1-inch heels

Finding your weight on the chart may be an eye-opening experience. If you're out of the range, then your physical wealth is 'in debt' and you need to make some investments in your body. This is just the beginning of your journey to creating, building, and maintaining your physical wealth.

Once you achieve your goals, you continue working on them. Just like your financial wealth, it is a life-long process to manage your health and continue building on it. As you age, there are different things to consider and physical wealth is dependent on you continuing to follow a healthy lifestyle.

Preventive testing at various ages becomes more important as we age. An annual check-up to identify early warning signs of potential health issues will help to ensure your physical wealth is as sound as it can be.

For example,

❖ yearly blood pressure and cholesterol screenings are recommended for all adults

❖ mammograms are recommended for women when they reach the age of 35 as a baseline for future years

❖ men and women are advised to have a colonoscopy at the age of 50 for early detection of cancer and to establish a baseline for the future

These types of tests are essential for ensuring your physical wealth. It's not just about exercise and nutrition – it's about total health management and building wealth that will pay off in years to come – just like your financial and mental wealth! Your doctor and health insurance carrier maintain a list of recommended preventive tests that are based on national clinical guidelines and they can help you establish a plan.

Knowing these important facts, you are now equipped with the information about your current health status and you know what you need to do for the future. You can move to step #3 in the process of accumulating your physical wealth.

3. Set your goals! Make a decision and mental commitment to change your lifestyle to reach your goals. That may include both exercise and nutritional changes.

4. Create a plan to meet your goals – just like you did to become debt-free! Start slowly by adding a 10-15 minute walk or other activity to your daily life. Increase 5-10 minutes each day until you are able to walk 45-60 minutes at least 4-5 times weekly.

   Your plan may include joining a gym. Do what you need to do to improve your physical fitness – but DO NOT go in debt to do it! If you don't have the money to join a gym, it's absolutely FREE to walk outdoors! Make decisions based on your financial situation.

   Make small, methodical changes in your diet. Start drinking more water daily. Eat smaller portions of foods you enjoy. Phase out foods that you know are bad for you. Take it slow and you will succeed – as long as you have a positive attitude, are persistent, and are equipped with a plan!

5. Reward yourself for small changes and for hitting milestones and targets. Your reward might be going to a movie, visiting a museum, or doing something to reward

both your physical and your mental self! After all, over half of the battle related to investing in your physical wealth is related to your mental wealth – they both deserve a reward!

Investing in your physical wealth is critical to all other aspects of your life. You must always commit to make changes mentally before you can really change your actions and make a difference. The mental wealth you have built is now giving you the stamina and motivation to invest in your body. Remember to always talk and think positively.

Positive self-talk and reinforcement is your strongest ally when it comes to making changes in your life.

If you stay focused positively, then you will be successful in whatever you set out to do!

The time and effort you put into taking care of your body and preparing for the days, weeks, and years ahead will pay off in many ways. But most importantly, it will give you peace of mind, a sense of well-being, and the ability to live simply and be simply happy.

Physical wealth is yours for life – it's something that no one else can take away from you except yourself.

Spiritual Wealth

We talk about four major capacities of life associated with 'wealth' in this book:

1. Financial wealth
2. Mental (emotional) wealth
3. Physical wealth
4. Spiritual wealth

All of these areas of your life are interrelated and interconnected in some way. How 'wealthy' you are in each area is most likely determined by your values and goals. When you approach life with goals that are incongruent with your values, you create confusion and anxiety for your body, your mind, and your life.

Conflicting values and goals can lead to unhappiness, insecurity, stress, depression, and both mental and physical illness. But when you establish goals that are driven by your true values, then you have greater harmony and peace in your life.

A harmonious life allows you to be simply happy. It enables you to tap into your innermost thoughts and the recesses of your mind to nourish your spirituality. This is an important aspect of your life and it is essential that you create spiritual wealth from which to draw wisdom, direction, and insights for your future.

It is unfortunate that people often spend all of their time and energy pursuing financial wealth and ignoring the important spiritual wealth they deserve. In the earlier sections of this book, we've explored the value and importance of attaining financial independence, mental wealth, and physical wealth. Once you are able to achieve these things, the result is a life that is simple and happy.

But there is MORE!

When you become satisfied and simply happy, you have a strong foundation on which to build your spiritual wealth. Consider the person who is struggling to pay bills and is totally unhappy with their job. They have little time to consider their spiritual health and their continuation at a rapid pace on the treadmill of life is robbing them of their spirituality.

That's why it is so important to strive for a life that is simply happy and debt-free. Then you have the ability to tap into your inner resources and reach your spirituality. Deepening your spirituality and strengthening your spiritual pursuit results in spiritual wealth that will feed your soul and mind for years to come.

Spiritual wealth defined

Everyone at some point in their life has experienced some type of spirituality. Consider the snow covered mountains, the rolling waves of the ocean, a field covered in daisies as far as the eye can see – these are the types of things can evoke spiritual feelings within people. Spiritual health can be a religious experience for some people and religion becomes a vital part of the lives.

Spiritual health is a critical element of human beings that leads to optimal health. The key to truly good health is to cultivate and exercise every dimension of health and create a healthy balance between them. That means cultivating your physical, mental, and spiritual health.

Cultivating and enhancing your spiritual health requires effort and it takes time and exercise. Just like conditioning your body, your mind must be conditioned as well. Spirituality comes from your ability to find a meaningful purpose for your life. Thinking about why you exist will help lead you to a more fulfilled life by giving your life meaning and purpose.

It will give you greater fulfillment when you know that you have made a difference in the world.

When you exercise your spiritual health and look inwardly at yourself, you will be happier and healthier. Having well-defined goals, a purpose in life, and strong values will help you cultivate your spirituality. Your spirituality builds on much of what you have already learned about discipline and caring for your physical and mental health.

People who have a healthy spiritual life find they are actually very wealthy! They form stronger bonds and relationships with other people. Healthy relationships strengthen spirituality for most people and the bonds they build with others enhances their ability to share and make a difference.

You cannot measure someone's spiritual health as you can their financial health. It is an intangible component of a person but it is a vital component. But when it comes to spiritual wealth, it is a part of your life that you do not want to neglect because it may bring more meaning to your life than anything else you can do.

Exploring spirituality

Spirituality is not something you can see or touch. It is not about objects or things. It is about self-reflection, meditation, and concentration. The best way to exercise and explore your spirituality is to find a quiet place where you can be undisturbed with your thoughts. The distractions of the world need to be temporarily shut out as you meditate on the things that give meaning to your life.

Some of the ways you can reach into your mind and begin exploring your spirituality include:

- Meditation
- Quietly thinking
- Practicing Yoga
- Praying

- Reading insightful books
- Listening to quiet music
- Watching a sunset

These types of activities will help you tap into your spirituality and you will be astounded at how good you feel when you consistently practice spiritual growth. It will enhance both your physical and your mental wealth and you'll be a much more fulfilled individual when all of your capacities work together.

Once you begin exploring your spirituality, you will actually find that your values and goals in life are much clearer to you. This will lead to a better alignment of values and goals. As we discussed earlier in this book, having your values and goals aligned well is what leads to mental wealth and ultimately financial wealth!

Spirituality is a gift

Your spirituality is a gift and when you use it wisely, you will find that it leads to a simply happy life. It sometimes provides you with a feeling of euphoria. You will have a much more positive outlook on life, stronger commitment to your values and goals, greater sense of internal peace, and higher levels of self-esteem. It is not something only for the masters of yoga, or gurus, or priests.

It is a gift offered to every human being and your job is to take it and cultivate it.

The most important thing for you to understand about spirituality is that is not magic! It is a part of the human spirit that enables you to live life to its fullest. Spirituality enables you to find answers to questions in the solitude of a moment. It does not only happen when you are meditating or praying – spirituality is with you every day, everywhere you go.

When you are trying to solve a complex problem or make a life-changing decision, your spirituality provides you with guidance and direction. Since it clarifies your values and makes them clearer and sharper, it helps you to make decisions that ultimately help you reach your goals.

You cannot define spiritual wealth in terms of dollars or other tangible measures. It essentially has no material value or worth. And it is also something that you cannot purchase. It comes from within you.

When you truly recognize your gift of spiritual wealth, you realize what is important to you in this life. You recognize that material possessions, jobs, and money are not the most important things to you. Spirituality enables you to focus on the things that you honestly value in life.

Ways to exercise spiritual wealth

Exploring spiritual wealth is the beginning but just like financial, physical, and mental wealth, it takes time to build a wealthy spiritual life. It takes a concentrated effort and commitment to stay focused. It is important to make time to enhance your spirituality to optimize your overall life experiences.

Consider these spiritual thoughts and how they can help you to focus your mind to cultivate your spirituality:

- Money can buy a house but not a home

- Money can buy books but not wisdom

- Money can buy medicine but not health

- Money can buy possessions but not peace

- Money can buy a diamond but not love

Spiritual wealth is important to your life because it helps you to understand what is important. Knowing what is important to you helps you determine what you really want to do in life. Asking yourself questions such as these will also aid you in exercising your spirituality:

❖ Do you want to help others?

❖ Do you want to spend more time with your family?

❖ Do you want to read more?

❖ Do you want to be more in touch with your inner self?

❖ Do you want to commune with God?

❖ Do you want to explore the environment more?

❖ Do you do enough to 'give back' to the world?

❖ Do you treat others as they should be treated?

❖ Do others see you as you see yourself?

The answers to these questions and other questions like them are often guided by your spirituality. It's a very personal matter and only you can determine the depth of your spirituality. Giving thoughtful consideration to questions like these will help you reach further into your mind to better understand your values.

When you do what you really want to do in life, you are happier and more fulfilled. If you pursue your passion in life and set your goals based on your values, then the money will follow. When you succeed at becoming debt-free and mentally wealthy, you can more fully explore life.

Keeping this in mind enables you to free your mind and focus more on your spirituality and the meaning of life.

> **The rewards of living a life that is financially, mentally, and physically wealthy will lead to a greater ability to achieve spiritual wealth.**

Spiritual wealth is your overall well-being and it is something that comes from within you. It's your spirit and it's waiting to be released by you. Allowing your spirituality to evolve and thrive gives your life more meaning and makes you more fulfilled.

You practice and cultivate spirituality every day of your life. Every decision you make can help you exercise this component of your life. Allow your spirituality to be your guide in situations such as the following:

- ❖ Find peace with the work you do every day. If that means changing jobs, changing professions, or going back to school – do what you truly desire to do based on your values. Find a job or work that makes you feel satisfied and fulfilled.

- ❖ Eliminate debt from your life. Don't allow unpaid bills and escalating debt to rob you of living the life you desire. Take control of your debt and your life. Your spirituality will help you determine what is most important to you and that will help you determine how to take control of your life.

❖ Take care of yourself – both mentally and physically. Participate in activities that reward you with a healthier body and mind. Practice Yoga or other meditation techniques to clear your mind and enable you to tap into your inner thoughts.

❖ Think positively and practice positive self-talk. It is true that positive self-talk is a self-fulfilling prophecy. You become what you believe you can become. Make sure that is positive! Continually talking positively to yourself has a tremendous impact on your actions and the results you achieve.

❖ Focus on the things in life that are important to you. Align your values and your goals and stay focused on the path to achieve them. Find happiness in your work and in your daily life. Let your spirituality be your guide. Meditate and think quietly about what is important and you will soon realize that the answer is right in front of you.

❖ Recognize that everyone has their own beliefs, values, and ideas. Don't force your ideas on others. And don't allow them to force their ideas and values on you. Stay true to your values. Just live your life the best way you know how. Be tolerant of other people and be empathetic towards their situations.

❖ Use relaxation techniques to steady your mind such as deep breathing. Think about the things in your life that have brought you joy. Create a list of things for which you are thankful. Use your quiet time and solitude to self-reflect.

❖ Pursue your dreams and goals. Follow your passion and your heart and create a plan to successfully get where you want to go. Stay true to your values and your dreams will come true.

❖ Express gratitude to other people. Your family, friends, and associates need to know you are grateful. The paper delivery person, the woman you meet in the elevator, the grocery store clerk – let them know you appreciate them and what they do for you and others. Gratitude should be one of your strongest allies! Expressing gratitude brings you great satisfaction and makes you feel wealthy. When you express gratitude, you are feeding and exercising your own spirituality.

❖ Meditate and read things which give you peace and satisfaction. Learn and study more about things that have meaning to you. Pass on your knowledge and information to other people. Share with others.

❖ Spend time alone to think and plan. Reflect on your life and the things you enjoy. Identify things that need work and make changes. Recognize your accomplishments and achievements and be thankful for them.

When you are able to focus on these types of activities and thoughts, then your spirituality will thrive. It will come alive and ignite your motivation and passion to continually strive to live the life you desire.

Live simply happy and let your spiritual wealth accumulate!

Spirituality helps create a simply happy life

Living simply happy is not always easy at first – the hustle and bustle of today's environment creates distractions and challenges. But when you are finally able to slow down and enjoy life, you will find that the simple life is a happy life. As you search for ways to simplify your life, reduce your debt, and take better care of yourself, things becomes clearer to you. Then, it becomes easier to be simply happy.

The simple life is not about wanting to accumulate more material possessions but it is about wanting to live a more fulfilling and rewarding life. It's about tapping into your spirituality for a greater sense of who you are and what's important in the world. When you are spiritually wealthy, you are able to step back and observe the beauty of the world and your life.

A life filled with spiritual wealth is a life filled with gratitude. Having gratitude for what you have, for other people, and for the day to day observations you make is the result of spirituality. It is also a life which allows time for you to walk a little slower and take time to appreciate the things you see, hear, touch, and smell.

When you become debt-free and are able to enjoy life by living the life you desire, then you are able to enjoy the very basics of life. That may be your family, your friends, a good book, helping a stranger, a stroll on the beach, a drive through the mountains, volunteering – whatever makes you happy and insightful.

The interconnectedness of your financial, mental, physical, and spiritual self becomes much clearer as you see how they intertwine in your life.

If your desire is to be debt-free and simply free, then that's the path you should take. That journey will lead to greater enlightenment and the ability to nourish your spirituality in ways you never thought possible.

The rewards will be great.

It may require some changes to the way you work and live. But it will give you the life you desire - including a quality of life that is rewarding and fulfilling. You will derive great satisfaction, fulfillment, and contentment from living the life you were meant to live.

Financial, mental, physical, and spiritual wealth

Our journey through this book has taken us through the four major capacities of your life. It's a never-ending, evolving circle of life that gives your life meaning and fulfillment. It takes all four capacities working together harmoniously for you to truly be wealthy in all aspects of your life.

1. The interconnectedness of the four capacities is much clearer now.

2. Finding peace with your financial situation leads to greater mental peace.

3. Mental peace provides you with the ability to take control of your life and your body. You are now able to improve and cultivate your physical health.

4. Being physically fit, mentally happy, and financially independent provides you with greater opportunity to explore your spiritual health and well-being.

Becoming wealthy in all aspects of your life should be your ultimate goal. Harmony between all four capacities will ensure that you are living the life you are meant to live. And that means living a life with purpose that is built on the foundation of your values.

Stockpiling material possessions, running on the treadmill of the rat-race every day, and neglecting the things that are most important to you becomes history. You are now able to sit back and enjoy life in ways beyond most people's comprehension – and you're doing it debt-free! Ironically, you are gaining more wealth every day than you ever did before.

Welcome to a wonderful new world that is simply happy and debt-free!

If one advances confidently in the direction of his dreams, and endeavors to live the life which he has imagined, he will meet with a success unexpected in common hours.

— Henry David Thoreau